YAKALOU MEDIA

Your Negative Self-talk Is Killing You

Here is: How, Why and What You Need To Do

Contents

Disclaimer   v

I   LET'S START HERE

Introduction   3
The 5 Rules to Get the Most Out of This Book   5
Word of Warning Before We Start   8
You Don't Have to Read It All—Start Where
You Need To   10

II   HERE IS: HOW, WHY AND WHAT YOU
NEED TO DO

Chapter 1: Damages Self-Esteem   15
Chapter 2: Blocks Success   20
Chapter 3: Increases Stress   25
Chapter 4: Limits Personal Growth   30
Chapter 5: Weakens Relationships   36
Chapter 6: Impacts Mental Health   42
Chapter 7: Affects Physical Health   48
Chapter 8: Reduces Resilience   54
Chapter 9: Skews Perception   60
Chapter 10: Creates a Negative Cycle   66
Now WHAT? You May Ask.   72

Disclaimer

This book is designed to provide information only. This information is provided and sold with the knowledge that the publisher and author do not offer any legal or other professional advice. In the case of a need for any such expertise, consult with the appropriate professional.

This book does not contain all the information available on the subject. This book has not been created to be specific to any individual's or organization's situation or needs. Every effort has been made to make this book as accurate as possible. However, there may be typographical and/or content errors. Therefore, this book should serve only as a general guide, not as the ultimate source of subject information.

This book contains information that might be dated and is intended only to educate and entertain. Regarding any loss or damage allegedly suffered or alleged to have occurred as a result of the information in this book, either directly or indirectly, the author and publisher shall have no liability or responsibility to any person or entity.

I

LET'S START HERE

Introduction

Do you ever hear a voice inside your head telling you that you're not good enough? Maybe it says you're not smart enough to succeed at work, or that you'll never reach your goals. This voice, often quiet but persistent, is your negative self-talk, and whether you realize it or not, it's shaping your life in ways you might not expect.

Have you ever wondered why you hold back from taking risks or pursuing your dreams? It's easy to blame external factors like time, money, or circumstances. But often, the real culprit is the way we talk to ourselves. Negative self-talk can be like an invisible barrier, stopping you from even trying. It tells you that you're going to fail before you begin, and over time, you start to believe it. How many opportunities have you let slip by because that voice told you not to bother?

Imagine what your life would look like if you could quiet that voice. Picture yourself stepping into a meeting without doubting your ideas, or waking up excited about your goals, confident that you can achieve them. How much lighter would you feel without the constant weight of self-criticism dragging you down? The truth is, you don't have to imagine. It's entirely possible to break free from the grip of negative self-talk—and this book will show you how.

But why does this matter? Because your potential is limitless, and it's time to stop letting self-doubt hold you back. Every day, you have the chance to create a life that's fulfilling and meaningful. The only thing standing in your way is the negative dialogue running through your mind. If you're ready to take control, stop sabotaging yourself, and unlock the best version of you, then this journey is for you.

Let's explore how this invisible enemy is slowly killing your confidence, your peace of mind, and your ability to live the life you deserve. You have the power to change the way you think about yourself, and that power starts with understanding how your self-talk shapes your reality. It's time to recognize the impact of these thoughts, face them head-on, and replace them with beliefs that empower you. Are you ready to silence the voice that's been holding you back?

The path to emotional freedom and reaching your full potential begins here.

The 5 Rules to Get the Most Out of This Book

You've picked up this book because something inside you knows it's time for a change. But how can you ensure that this journey is truly transformative? How can you walk away from these pages not just inspired, but empowered to take real action in your life? The answer lies in how you approach what you're about to read. Just like with anything in life, the effort you put in will shape the results you get. So, let's start by setting some simple, but powerful, ground rules to guide you through this book and get the most out of every page.

Rule 1: Be Honest With Yourself

Before anything else, commit to being honest with yourself. This book is designed to challenge the way you think and talk to yourself. Some of it may be uncomfortable—after all, facing your own inner dialogue can be tough. But here's the thing: if you're not willing to look closely at your thoughts and acknowledge the ways they might be holding you back, change won't happen. Ask yourself: Are you ready to be open and truthful, even when it's hard? Honesty is the foundation for growth, and the more honest you are, the more you'll gain from this process.

Rule 2: Keep an Open Mind

It's easy to assume you already know everything about your habits, thoughts, and beliefs. But if you come into this with a closed mind, you'll miss opportunities to discover new ways of thinking. Think of this book as a conversation with yourself, one where curiosity is key. Be open to ideas that may feel unfamiliar or even uncomfortable at first. Remember, real change often comes from stepping outside of what feels safe and predictable. Ask yourself: What if the way you've been thinking is only part of the story? What if there's a better way forward?

Rule 3: Take Action, Don't Just Read

This book isn't just a collection of ideas—it's a guide for action. To truly benefit, you need to do more than just read; you need to apply the lessons to your own life. As you move through each chapter, make a commitment to pause and reflect. Try out the strategies, even if they feel challenging at first. Real change comes from action, not just understanding. Think about it: How different could your life be if you took just one small step each day to shift your self-talk? This book gives you the tools, but it's up to you to use them.

Rule 4: Be Patient With Yourself

Change doesn't happen overnight. As you start to work through your negative self-talk, you may find yourself slipping back into old habits. That's okay—it's part of the process. Be patient with yourself, and remember that progress is rarely a straight line. The key is persistence, not perfection. Every small step forward is a victory, even if it doesn't feel like it in the moment. Ask yourself: Can you be kind to yourself along the way? The goal isn't to be perfect; it's to make consistent, meaningful progress.

Rule 5: Stay Committed

Finally, the most important rule of all: stay committed. It's easy to start a book like this with enthusiasm, but lasting change requires dedication. As you read, you'll likely encounter moments where you feel challenged or even frustrated. Don't let those moments stop you. Push through them, and remind yourself why you started this journey in the first place. You're here because you want to live a better, more fulfilling life. Don't lose sight of that. Think about this: How will your life look in six months, a year, or even five years if you stick with this? The potential for transformation is limitless, but only if you see it through.

By following these five rules—being honest, staying open-minded, taking action, being patient, and staying committed—you're setting yourself up for success. These aren't just rules for getting through the book; they're guidelines for creating real change in your life. The journey starts now. Are you ready to get the most out of it?

Word of Warning Before We Start

Before we dive in, let's pause for a moment. You've picked up this book because you want something to change—maybe it's the way you think, the way you feel, or the way you live. That's a powerful decision, and I'm here to help guide you. But before we begin, there's a word of warning you need to hear.

This book will challenge you. It's going to ask you to look closely at the thoughts you have about yourself, thoughts you may have carried for years. Some of these thoughts might be so ingrained that you believe they're true without question. And here's the tricky part: changing them won't always feel easy or comfortable. Are you prepared to face the voice inside your head that's been telling you "you're not enough" for far too long?

If you're expecting a quick fix, you might want to reconsider. Personal growth is a process, and it takes time. There will be moments when you're tempted to give up, to return to the comfort of familiar habits, even if those habits are the very things holding you back. You might wonder if it's worth the effort, or worse, you may convince yourself that change isn't possible for you. But here's the truth: it absolutely is. The question isn't whether you can change, but whether you're willing to stick with it when the road gets rough.

Think of it this way: if your negative self-talk has been part of your life for years, it won't just vanish overnight. It will take patience and practice to rewire the way you speak to yourself. There will be setbacks. You may feel like you're not making progress, even when you are. But every step forward, no matter how small, is a victory. And those victories will add up—if you're willing to keep going.

You also need to know that this journey isn't just about eliminating negative thoughts; it's about learning to replace them with something better. Silence alone isn't enough. You need to build a new voice inside your head, one that encourages, supports, and motivates you. This requires effort and awareness. Are you ready to become your own biggest supporter, rather than your harshest critic?

Let's be clear: this isn't a path for the faint-hearted. But you're not here because you want things to stay the same. You're here because you're ready for change, even if it's hard. So, before we start, ask yourself this: Are you truly ready to let go of the thoughts that are holding you back? Are you prepared to face the discomfort that comes with growth? If the answer is yes, then you're in the right place.

This book will guide you, but you have to be willing to do the work. The change you seek is real and possible—but it's up to you to make it happen. Ready to begin? Let's go.

You Don't Have to Read It All—Start Where You Need To

Here's some good news: you don't have to read this book from cover to cover. In fact, you don't even have to finish it at all. This isn't the kind of book where you need to absorb every single word to make progress. You can jump around, pick the sections that speak to you in the moment, and start there. Think of it as a toolkit—each chapter offers something different, and you can take what you need when you need it.

We all have days where we're struggling with a specific challenge. Maybe today, you're dealing with overwhelming self-doubt. Tomorrow, you might feel frustrated with a habit you just can't break. The beauty of this book is that it's designed to meet you where you are. If you're feeling stuck on a particular issue, flip to the chapter that addresses it. Start with the questions that resonate with you in that moment, and you'll find what you need to get unstuck.

Life isn't linear, and neither is personal growth. You might not always be in the mood for deep reflection or heavy topics. Some days, you'll want to dig into the tough stuff; other days, you'll just want a small win to keep moving forward. That's why this book is structured to give you flexibility. You don't have to follow a set path. Let your own feelings guide you.

Remember, this is your journey. Whether you're reading one page or ten, you're still making progress. So, go ahead and skip around. Don't feel pressured to follow a rigid plan—just start where it feels right.

II

HERE IS: HOW, WHY AND WHAT YOU NEED TO DO

Chapter 1: Damages Self-Esteem

Constantly Criticizing Yourself

The Story of Sarah

Sarah sat at her desk, staring blankly at her computer screen. Another email had just come in from her boss, pointing out a small mistake she'd made in her report. Even though the error wasn't a big deal, Sarah felt her heart sink. This was just another sign, she thought, that she wasn't good enough. "Why can't I ever get things right?" she muttered under her breath.

Lately, this had become a daily routine for Sarah. Each time she encountered even the smallest setback, her mind would spiral. She replayed her mistakes over and over again, convincing herself that she was failing at everything—her job, her relationships, even her personal goals. When she looked in the mirror, she saw someone unworthy and incapable. Little did she know, her constant self-criticism was the root of the problem.

Have you ever felt like Sarah? Do you find yourself focusing on your faults, no matter how minor they are, until they start to define how you see yourself? If so, you're not alone. Many people fall into the trap of negative self-talk, and over time, it can seriously damage your self-esteem. But how exactly does this happen? And more importantly, how can you stop it before it causes more harm?

How Criticism Eats Away at Your Confidence

It starts small. Maybe you make a simple mistake at work, miss a deadline, or say something awkward in a conversation. Instead of brushing it off and moving on, you start to replay the moment in your head. "I can't believe I did that. I'm so stupid," you think. Soon, these thoughts turn into a habit. You don't even notice how often you're criticizing yourself, but each time you do, it chips away at your self-esteem.

Why does this happen? Our brains are wired to remember negative experiences more easily than positive ones—it's part of our survival instinct. But when we let negative thoughts dominate, they begin to shape how we see ourselves. If all you focus on are your flaws and failures, it's no surprise that you start to believe that's all you are. And when you start seeing yourself this way, it becomes harder to see your strengths, your potential, and your worth.

But here's an important question: What happens when you believe you're unworthy or incapable?

Why It Hurts Your Progress

When you're constantly putting yourself down, it's like trying to build a house with broken tools. Self-criticism undermines your ability to grow and achieve your goals. Why? Because when you don't believe in yourself, you stop trying. You avoid challenges, fearing that you'll fail. You second-guess your decisions, feeling paralyzed by doubt. And even when you succeed, you dismiss your accomplishments as "luck" or "no big deal."

It's a vicious cycle. The more you criticize yourself, the more your confidence shrinks. The smaller your confidence gets, the harder it is to take risks, try new things, or believe you can improve. And when you stop believing in your potential, you stop living up to it.

But here's the good news: You can break this cycle. It's not easy, but it's possible. So, how do you start?

What You Need to Do to Change

The first step is awareness. Pay attention to the way you talk to yourself. Are your thoughts supportive or critical? Start noticing the moments when you're putting yourself down. For example, the next time you catch yourself thinking, "I always mess things up," pause. Ask yourself: Is that really true? Do I *always* mess things up? The answer is likely no.

Now that you're aware, the next step is to challenge those negative thoughts. Instead of letting them control your mindset, question them. Replace self-criticism with more balanced thoughts. Let's say you made a mistake at work. Instead of saying, "I'm so bad at this," try saying, "I made a mistake, but I can learn from it." Do you see the difference? One thought tears you down, while the other builds you up.

You can also shift your focus toward your strengths. What are you good at? What are the things you've accomplished that you're proud of? Writing them down can help remind you of your worth. The goal isn't to ignore your flaws—it's to acknowledge them without letting them define you.

Building a Positive Inner Dialogue

Change won't happen overnight, and that's okay. It takes practice. Start small by catching yourself when negative thoughts creep in. Then, slowly begin to replace those thoughts with more positive, constructive ones. Be patient with yourself during this process—after all, this is about building yourself up, not tearing yourself down for not changing fast enough.

So, are you ready to give yourself the same kindness and encouragement you'd offer a friend? Imagine how your life might change if, instead of being your worst critic, you became your biggest supporter. How would your confidence grow? What could you achieve if you truly believed in yourself?

It's time to stop letting self-criticism hold you back. You deserve better than the negative story you've been telling yourself.

Reflection Questions:

1. When was the last time you criticized yourself for something small? How did it make you feel?
2. What are three strengths you have that you often overlook?
3. How would your life be different if you were kinder to yourself?
4. When you make a mistake, what's the first thought that comes to your mind? How can you challenge it?
5. What is one positive thing you can say to yourself today?

Practical Exercise:

Write down three recent situations where you criticized yourself. For each situation, write an alternative thought that is kinder and more supportive. For example, if you thought, "I'm not good at my job," replace it with, "I made a mistake, but I'm learning and improving." Keep this list visible and refer to it whenever you catch yourself engaging in negative self-talk.

Chapter 2: Blocks Success

Negative Self-Talk Prevents You from Reaching Your Full Potential

The Story of Michael

Michael had always dreamed of starting his own business. For years, he talked about opening a small cafe in his neighborhood, imagining the scent of freshly brewed coffee and the sound of customers chatting happily over their meals. But every time he sat down to make a plan, his mind flooded with doubt. "What if I fail? What if no one shows up? I'm not good enough to run a business."

Instead of moving forward, Michael stayed in his comfortable but unsatisfying job. He watched others take the risks he was too afraid to take. He scrolled through social media, seeing posts about people who had started their own businesses and succeeded, feeling a sharp pang of jealousy and regret. Deep down, he knew he was holding himself back—but he couldn't seem to break free from his negative thoughts.

Have you ever found yourself in Michael's shoes? You have big dreams, but you keep telling yourself that you're not good enough, that you'll fail, or that it's too risky to even try? If so, you've already felt the power of negative self-talk to block your success. But why does this happen, and what can you do to stop it?

How Negative Self-Talk Sabotages Your Success

When you tell yourself you can't succeed, you set yourself up to fail before you've even begun. It's like trying to climb a mountain with a backpack full of rocks. Every step is harder because you've already convinced yourself you won't make it to the top. This mindset doesn't just affect how you feel—it influences what you do.

For instance, imagine you're about to give a big presentation at work. If you walk in thinking, "I'm terrible at this, no one will be impressed," how will you perform? You'll likely feel nervous, fumble your words, and overlook key points. But the worst part? You won't see it as a learning opportunity—you'll see it as proof that you were right all along: "I'm just not cut out for this."

This creates a cycle. The more you think you can't succeed, the less effort you put into trying, and the less likely you are to succeed. Every setback becomes "evidence" that you weren't good enough in the first place, reinforcing your negative beliefs. It's a form of self-sabotage that happens so quietly, you might not even realize it's happening.

But have you ever stopped to wonder: What could happen if you removed that voice of doubt? What would your life look like if you believed success was possible?

Why You're Sabotaging Yourself

Our minds are powerful, and sometimes, they work against us. Negative self-talk often comes from a fear of failure. If you tell yourself you can't succeed, you give yourself an excuse not to try. It feels safer that way—if you don't try, you can't fail, right? But here's the catch: You're also blocking any chance of success.

Think about it. Every time you doubt yourself, you're closing the door to opportunities. You're saying "no" to possibilities before they even present themselves. And over time, this mindset becomes a habit. You become so used to telling yourself you're not good enough that it becomes your default mode of thinking.

But what if you challenged that habit? What if, instead of asking, "What if I fail?" you asked, "What if I succeed?" How would that change your approach to the things you care about?

What You Can Do to Break Free

The first step to overcoming self-sabotage is recognizing when it's happening. The next time you catch yourself thinking, "I can't do this," pause. Ask yourself: Where is this thought coming from? Is it based on facts, or is it just fear talking? More often than not, it's fear disguised as logic.

Once you've identified the negative thought, challenge it. Let's say you're afraid to apply for a promotion because you think you're not qualified. Instead of dwelling on that fear, look at the facts. Have you completed similar tasks before? Do you have the skills required? Can you learn what you don't yet know? Replace "I'm not good enough" with "I have the ability to learn and grow."

Another powerful tool is visualization. Picture yourself succeeding. Close your eyes and imagine what it looks like to achieve your goals. What does success feel like? What does it sound like? Visualizing success can help rewire your brain to focus on what's possible instead of what could go wrong.

But here's the most important part: Take action. Even if it's a small step, do something today that moves you closer to your goal. Action is the antidote to doubt. The more you try, the more you'll prove to yourself that success isn't as out of reach as you thought.

Turning Fear into Motivation

One of the most surprising things you'll discover as you begin to challenge negative self-talk is that the fear of failure can be transformed into motivation. Instead of letting fear stop you, use it as fuel to push forward. What's the worst that could happen? You try, and it doesn't work out? That's not the end—it's a learning experience that brings you one step closer to success.

Michael, for example, eventually realized that his fear of failure had been holding him back. He decided to take the leap and start small, opening a weekend pop-up cafe. At first, not everything went perfectly—there were slow days and a few mistakes along the way. But instead of seeing those as failures, Michael viewed them as lessons. Slowly but surely, his confidence grew. And as his belief in himself strengthened, so did his business.

What about you? Are you ready to stop sabotaging your own success? The path forward isn't without challenges, but if you stop letting your fears control you, there's no telling how far you can go.

Reflection Questions:

1. When was the last time you told yourself you couldn't do something? How did it affect your actions?
2. What is one big goal you've been avoiding because of self-doubt?
3. How would your life change if you started believing in your ability to succeed?
4. What's the worst that could happen if you tried and didn't succeed? What would you learn from that experience?
5. How can you start challenging your negative thoughts today?

Practical Exercise:

Take one small step toward a goal you've been avoiding due to self-doubt. It doesn't have to be big—just something that moves you forward. Write down what you did and how it made you feel. Reflect on whether your fear was justified or if it was holding you back unnecessarily. Keep track of your progress, and notice how each small action helps build your confidence over time.

Chapter 3: Increases Stress

How Self-Criticism Triggers Anxiety and Harms Your Well-Being

The Story of Emma

Emma sat on her couch, clutching her phone, anxiously reading over an email from her boss. There was no harsh criticism in the message—just some feedback on how she could improve a recent project. But to Emma, it felt like an attack. Her heart raced, her palms got sweaty, and she started replaying every tiny mistake she'd made on that project. "How could I have been so careless?" she thought. "I'm such a failure."

This wasn't the first time Emma felt this way. In fact, these stressful episodes had become part of her daily life. Every time she made a mistake or received feedback, her mind spiraled into self-criticism. The stress from constantly worrying about her performance and doubting her abilities had started to affect her health—headaches, difficulty sleeping, and constant tension in her shoulders.

Have you ever felt like Emma? Maybe you've had moments where one critical thought led to a cascade of worry, making you feel overwhelmed and anxious. Self-criticism, though it may seem harmless at first, can be a major source of stress. But why does it have such a powerful effect on us, and how can we stop it from taking over our lives?

How Self-Criticism Triggers Stress

When you criticize yourself, your brain reacts the same way it would if you were facing a real danger. It activates the "fight-or-flight" response—your heart rate speeds up, your muscles tense, and your body releases stress hormones like cortisol. This response is designed to protect you from physical threats, but when it's triggered by self-criticism, there's no real danger to run from. Instead, you're left with all the physical symptoms of stress and no way to relieve them.

Over time, this constant activation of the stress response wears your body down. You might start to notice physical symptoms like headaches, fatigue, or an upset stomach. Mentally, chronic stress can make you feel anxious, irritable, and overwhelmed. You may even begin to avoid situations that could trigger more self-criticism, which can limit your growth and happiness.

But here's the big question: If self-criticism is creating so much stress, why do we keep doing it?

Why We Keep Criticizing Ourselves

Self-criticism often comes from a desire to do better or to avoid mistakes. We think that by being hard on ourselves, we'll push ourselves to improve. But this belief is misguided. Instead of motivating us, constant self-criticism creates a cycle of stress and anxiety that makes it harder to think clearly, solve problems, or make decisions.

Wanting to fit in or gain acceptance from others is another reason why we criticize ourselves. We think that if we point out our flaws before anyone else does, we'll somehow protect ourselves from judgment. But here's the thing: Criticizing yourself doesn't protect you—it just makes you feel worse. And the more you engage in negative self-talk, the more stressed and anxious you become, which only reinforces the cycle.

So, if self-criticism is causing so much harm, how can you break free from it?

What You Need to Do to Reduce Stress

Recognizing when self-criticism is occurring is the first step in reducing stress that it causes. Pay attention to the thoughts that run through your mind when you're feeling anxious or stressed. Are you focusing on your flaws? Are you telling yourself you're not good enough? Once you become aware of these thoughts, you can begin to change them.

One effective way to combat self-criticism is through self-compassion. Instead of beating yourself up for making a mistake, treat yourself with the same kindness you'd offer a friend. Imagine if a close friend came to you feeling anxious after a mistake at work. Would you tell them they're a failure? Of course not. You'd reassure them, help them see the mistake as a learning opportunity, and remind them of their strengths. Why not offer that same support to yourself?

Another helpful tool is mindfulness. When you feel stress building up, pause and focus on your breath. Mindfulness helps you stay present in the moment rather than getting lost in negative thoughts about the past or future. It's a way to break the cycle of self-criticism before it spirals into full-blown anxiety.

Replacing Criticism with Positive Action

Instead of letting self-criticism lead to stress, turn it into an opportunity for growth. Ask yourself: What can I learn from this situation? How can I improve without tearing myself down in the process?

For example, if you didn't perform well in a meeting, instead of thinking, "I'm terrible at presentations," try thinking, "I didn't do my best today, but next time I'll prepare differently." This shift in thinking helps you focus on solutions rather than problems, reducing the stress that comes from constant self-blame.

Additionally, taking care of your physical health can help reduce the impact of stress. Exercise, even something as simple as a walk, can lower your cortisol levels and release endorphins, which improve your mood. Sleep is another crucial factor—without enough rest, your brain is more likely to fall into patterns of negativity and anxiety.

But perhaps the most important thing to remember is that progress takes time. Reducing stress from self-criticism doesn't happen overnight. It's a process of learning to be kinder to yourself, to take a step back when stress hits, and to choose positive action over self-doubt.

Moving Toward a Calmer, Healthier Life

Imagine what your life could look like if you stopped letting self-criticism control you. Think about the relief you would feel if you could face challenges without that constant, nagging voice telling you you're not good enough. How would your stress levels change if you gave yourself permission to make mistakes and learn from them without judgment?

By reducing the power of self-criticism, you're not just protecting your mental and physical health—you're opening the door to a life with less stress and more joy. It's a journey, but one worth taking. After all, you deserve to feel calm, confident, and capable, not weighed down by anxiety and doubt.

Reflection Questions:

1. When do you most often criticize yourself? How does it affect your stress levels?
2. Can you think of a recent time when self-criticism caused you unnecessary anxiety? How could you have handled it differently?
3. What are some physical signs that you're feeling stressed? How can you address them before they escalate?
4. How would your life change if you practiced more self-compassion?
5. What one simple action can you take right now to lessen the stress that comes from self-criticism?

Practical Exercise:

The next time you catch yourself engaging in self-criticism, pause and take a deep breath. Write down the critical thought you had. Then, write a kinder, more compassionate version of that thought. For example, if you thought, "I'm always making mistakes," rewrite it as, "I made a mistake, but I'm learning and growing." Keep this list of compassionate responses handy, and refer to it whenever you feel stress building up from negative self-talk. Over time, notice how this practice affects your stress levels.

Chapter 4: Limits Personal Growth

How Focusing on Your Flaws Stops You from Moving Forward

The Story of James

James had always been a bright student, but as he grew older, something changed. He became more cautious—hesitant, even—about trying new things. He'd often catch himself thinking, "I'm just not smart enough for this," or "What if I mess up and everyone notices?" Because of these thoughts, he stayed in his comfort zone, avoiding opportunities that could have helped him grow. When his company announced a training program for leadership skills, he didn't sign up. When a friend invited him to join a networking event, he politely declined.

Years passed, and James found himself stuck in the same role, watching colleagues move ahead while he stayed behind. He often felt frustrated, wondering why he wasn't advancing like everyone else. But deep down, he knew the answer: It was his own negative self-talk. By constantly focusing on what he believed were his shortcomings, he had created a barrier between himself and his personal and professional growth.

Does James's story sound familiar? Have you ever avoided

challenges or passed up new opportunities because you didn't believe you were capable? If so, you're not alone. Many people fall into the trap of letting self-criticism limit their growth. But how exactly does this happen, and what can you do to change it?

How Focusing on Flaws Limits Your Potential

When you focus on your perceived flaws, it's like looking at life through a distorted lens. Instead of seeing opportunities for growth and learning, all you see are the reasons why you can't succeed. "I'm not good at public speaking," you tell yourself, so you avoid presentations. "I'm not a natural leader," you think, so you pass on leadership roles. Every flaw you focus on becomes a wall that stops you from moving forward.

The problem with this way of thinking is that it doesn't give you the chance to improve. If you never step outside your comfort zone, you never learn new skills. And without learning, there's no room for personal growth. You stay stuck in the same place, feeling frustrated and unfulfilled.

But here's something to think about: What if your flaws aren't permanent? What if, instead of being roadblocks, they were simply areas for improvement? How would that change the way you approach new challenges?

Why We Avoid Challenges

There's a reason why focusing on flaws makes us avoid challenges—it's easier to stick with what's comfortable. Trying something new means taking a risk. There's always a chance you might fail or look foolish, and that can be scary. So, we tell ourselves it's safer to stay where we are. We convince ourselves that we don't have what it takes, so why bother trying?

But here's the thing: Growth doesn't happen in your comfort

zone. It happens when you push yourself to try something new, even if you're not sure you'll succeed. Every successful person has faced challenges, made mistakes, and learned from them. The difference is that they didn't let their fear of failure hold them back.

So, ask yourself: What's more important—staying comfortable, or reaching your full potential?

How to Break Free and Start Growing

The first step to overcoming the limits of self-criticism is shifting your mindset. Instead of focusing on your perceived flaws, start thinking about your potential. You don't have to be perfect to grow. You just have to be willing to try.

One powerful way to do this is by embracing a "growth mindset." According to this idea, which psychologist Carol Dweck developed, people with a growth mindset think they can improve their abilities through effort, education, and perseverance. In contrast, those with a "fixed mindset" believe their talents are set in stone, which leads them to avoid challenges for fear of failure.

Think about it this way: When you tell yourself, "I'm not good at this," you're adopting a fixed mindset. But if you say, "I can get better at this with practice," you're embracing a growth mindset. This small shift in thinking can make a huge difference in how you approach challenges.

Here's an example: Let's say you're asked to lead a project at work, but your first thought is, "I've never done this before—I'm not cut out for leadership." Instead of turning down the opportunity, try reframing the thought: "I've never done this before, but it's a chance to learn and grow." Suddenly, the challenge becomes less about your flaws and more about your potential.

The Power of Taking Small Steps

Another key to personal growth is to take small, manageable steps. You don't have to leap into the deep end right away. Start by challenging yourself in small ways. Maybe you take on a new task at work that pushes you just a little bit outside your comfort zone. Or perhaps you sign up for a class that teaches a skill you've always wanted to learn.

The important thing is to keep moving forward. Every small success builds your confidence and helps you see that your flaws aren't as limiting as you thought. Over time, you'll develop the skills and mindset needed to tackle bigger challenges.

But remember, growth is a process. It's okay to stumble along the way. What matters is that you're making progress, not that you're perfect.

Stop Comparing Yourself to Others

Another trap that limits personal growth is comparing yourself to others. When you focus on your flaws, it's easy to look at other people's successes and feel like you'll never measure up. "She's such a natural at this," you think. "Why can't I be like that?"

The truth is, everyone is on their own journey. Just because someone else seems to excel in a certain area doesn't mean you're not capable of success. The key is to focus on your own path. What skills do you want to develop? What goals do you want to achieve? Instead of comparing yourself to others, use their successes as inspiration for what's possible.

Ask yourself: What would happen if you stopped worrying about what others are doing and started focusing on your own growth?

Moving Forward with Confidence

At the end of the day, limiting your personal growth by focusing on your flaws is like staying in a cage with the door wide open. You have the power to step out and explore new possibilities—you just need to believe you can.

So, what would your life look like if you stopped letting self-criticism hold you back? How would you feel if you took on challenges with confidence, knowing that you have the ability to learn and grow?

The path to personal growth isn't always easy, but it's worth it. And the good news is that every step you take brings you closer to your full potential. The question is: Are you ready to take that first step?

Reflection Questions:

1. What challenges have you avoided because you focused on your flaws?
2. How would your life change if you believed your abilities could improve with effort?
3. What is one new skill or challenge you'd like to take on, but have been too afraid to try?
4. How can you reframe a negative thought about yourself into a growth-focused one?
5. When was the last time you compared yourself to someone else? How did it make you feel?

Practical Exercise:

Choose one small challenge you've been avoiding due to self-doubt. It could be anything—speaking up in a meeting, trying a new hobby, or taking on a project at work. Commit to taking one small step toward it. After you've taken the step, write down how it felt to push past your fear and what you learned from the experience. Keep track of your progress and celebrate each small victory as you move forward.

Chapter 5: Weakens Relationships

How Negative Self-Talk Erodes Trust and Connection

The Story of Lisa

Lisa had always been a thoughtful and caring friend. She went out of her way to support the people she loved, but lately, things felt different. She started doubting whether her friends truly valued her. When she didn't get a reply to a text or wasn't invited to an outing, she assumed it was because they didn't like her anymore. "I must have said something wrong," she thought. "Maybe I'm just not a good friend."

These thoughts played on repeat in Lisa's mind, making her feel insecure and anxious about her relationships. She became distant, responding less in group chats, and when she did meet with friends, she felt awkward and on edge. The more she convinced herself that she wasn't worthy of their friendship, the more strained her relationships became. Soon, her friends noticed something was off, leading to misunderstandings and growing tension.

Have you ever felt like Lisa—constantly questioning your worth in your relationships? Do you assume the worst when you don't get an immediate response from a loved one, or when plans change suddenly? If so, you've experienced how negative self-talk can weaken your relationships, not just with others, but with yourself. Let's explore how this happens and, more importantly, what you can do to stop it.

How Negative Self-Talk Damages Relationships

When you engage in negative self-talk, it doesn't just affect your self-esteem—it can also damage your relationships. Here's why: If you're constantly telling yourself that you're not good enough, you start believing that others must feel the same way. You may interpret their actions through the lens of insecurity, assuming that every missed text, every canceled plan, is a sign that they don't care about you or don't value your relationship.

But here's the thing—most of the time, these thoughts are far from the truth. People have busy lives, distractions, and their own struggles, and often, their actions have nothing to do with you. However, when negative self-talk is in control, it's hard to see things clearly. You might start to withdraw, become overly sensitive, or even create conflict where none exists.

Have you ever jumped to conclusions about a friend or partner's behavior? How often have those conclusions been accurate?

Why Negative Self-Talk Leads to Insecurity

Insecurity is one of the most destructive effects of negative self-talk. When you constantly criticize yourself, you build a story in your mind that you're unworthy of love, respect, or attention. This insecurity makes you question the strength of your relationships. Instead of feeling confident in the bonds you've built with others, you're always waiting for the other shoe to drop, expecting rejection or betrayal.

This insecurity can lead to misunderstandings. For example, if a friend doesn't respond to a message right away, you might think, "They must be upset with me," when in reality, they're just busy. You might start sending follow-up messages, anxiously asking if everything is okay, which can make your friend feel pressured or confused. This, in turn, can create unnecessary conflict and strain.

The sad irony is that the very thoughts meant to protect you from being hurt—like "I'm not good enough for them" or "They'll leave me eventually"—end up causing the hurt you were trying to avoid. By expecting rejection, you might start acting in ways that push people away, creating a self-fulfilling prophecy.

So, how can you stop this cycle of insecurity and rebuild trust in your relationships?

What You Can Do to Strengthen Your Relationships

The first step in breaking free from the grip of negative self-talk is to become aware of it. Start paying attention to your thoughts, especially when you feel anxious or insecure in your relationships. Are you assuming the worst? Are you telling yourself that you're not valued or loved? Once you identify these thoughts, you can begin to challenge them.

One way to challenge negative self-talk is to ask yourself: *Is this thought based on facts, or is it just a fear I have?* For example, if you think, "My friend is ignoring me because they don't like me anymore," take a step back and ask, "Do I have any real evidence to support this?" Most of the time, you'll find that your fears are based on assumptions, not reality.

Another helpful strategy is to communicate openly with the people in your life. Instead of letting insecurity build up in your mind, talk to your friend or partner about how you're feeling. For example, if you're worried that a friend is upset with you, ask them directly but calmly: "Hey, I noticed you've been quiet lately. Is everything okay between us?" Most of the time, you'll find that their actions had nothing to do with you, and having that conversation will ease your mind.

Lastly, remind yourself of your value in your relationships. Make a list of the qualities that make you a good friend or partner—whether it's your loyalty, sense of humor, or willingness to help. Reflecting on your strengths can help counteract the negative thoughts that make you feel unworthy.

But what if your negative self-talk is so deeply ingrained that it feels impossible to shake?

The Long-Term Impact of Self-Criticism on Relationships

If negative self-talk goes unchecked, it can cause lasting damage to your relationships. Over time, your constant self-criticism can erode trust, not just with others but with yourself. You might start second-guessing every interaction, wondering if you've said or done something wrong, even when nothing is wrong at all. This kind of mental strain can make it hard to relax and enjoy your relationships.

For example, imagine you're at a gathering with friends, and someone makes a lighthearted joke. If you're feeling insecure, you might interpret the joke as an attack on you, even if it wasn't meant that way. Instead of laughing along, you pull back emotionally, convinced that your friends don't really like you. This kind of misunderstanding can lead to distance in relationships, making it harder to maintain strong connections.

But the good news is that you can change. By recognizing when negative self-talk is affecting your relationships, you can take steps to rebuild trust and strengthen your connections. The key is to practice self-compassion and give yourself the benefit of the doubt. After all, your friends and loved ones are in your life for a reason—they see your worth, even when you don't.

Moving Forward with Trust and Confidence

Imagine what your relationships would look like if you stopped doubting yourself. Picture yourself feeling secure in your friendships, trusting that the people in your life care about you because of who you are, not in spite of your flaws. What would happen if, instead of assuming the worst, you trusted that your relationships were strong enough to handle the ups and downs?

By reducing negative self-talk, you can not only improve your self-esteem but also create deeper, more fulfilling relationships. It takes time and practice, but by challenging your negative thoughts and communicating openly, you can build stronger bonds and feel more secure in the relationships that matter most.

Reflection Questions:

1. When was the last time you assumed the worst in a relationship? How did that assumption affect your behavior?
2. What insecurities do you often bring into your relationships, and how can you challenge them?
3. How would your relationships change if you trusted that you were worthy of love and friendship?
4. When you feel insecure, how do you usually react? How could you respond differently next time?

5. What is one way you can communicate more openly with your loved ones when you're feeling uncertain?

Practical Exercise:

The next time you feel insecure in a relationship, pause and write down the thought that's making you feel anxious. Then, write down an alternative explanation for the situation. For example, if you think, "My friend didn't text me back because they don't care," replace it with, "My friend is probably busy, and it doesn't mean they don't care about me." Keep a journal of these thoughts and revisit them when you start to feel insecure. Over time, this practice will help you build more trust in your relationships.

Chapter 6: Impacts Mental Health

How Persistent Negativity Can Lead to Depression and Anxiety

The Story of Mark

Mark used to be the life of the party. He was outgoing, always cracking jokes, and had a strong circle of friends. But over the past year, something changed. He started feeling overwhelmed by the smallest things—an offhand comment from a coworker, a minor mistake at work, or even just scrolling through social media. It was as if a constant cloud of negativity hung over him, no matter what he did.

"Why am I like this?" Mark would think. "I'm never going to be as good as everyone else." Slowly, he started withdrawing from his friends, isolating himself, and spending long hours lying in bed, scrolling through his phone, and feeling increasingly detached. The things that once brought him joy now felt exhausting, and the more he tried to pull himself out of it, the deeper he seemed to sink.

Eventually, Mark was diagnosed with anxiety and depression. Looking back, he realized that it hadn't happened overnight. His struggle with persistent negativity had been growing over time, slowly eating away at his mental health until it became too heavy to bear.

Does Mark's story resonate with you? Have you ever found yourself caught in a spiral of negative thoughts that seem impossible to escape? While occasional self-doubt or frustration is normal, persistent negativity can have a serious impact on your mental health, leading to conditions like depression and anxiety. But how does this happen, and what steps can you take to protect your mental well-being?

How Negative Self-Talk Affects Your Mental Health

When negative self-talk becomes a constant part of your internal dialogue, it can profoundly affect how you see yourself and the world around you. At first, it might seem like just an annoyance—a passing thought that says, "I'm not good enough" or "I'll never get this right." But when those thoughts show up day after day, they begin to shape your reality.

Negative thoughts are like seeds. The more you allow them to take root, the more they grow and spread. Soon, a single self-critical thought can evolve into a mindset of hopelessness or helplessness, where you feel powerless to change your situation. Over time, this persistent negativity can contribute to mental health disorders such as depression and anxiety.

But why does negative self-talk have such a strong impact on your mental health? Let's break it down.

Why Persistent Negativity Leads to Depression and Anxiety

Our brains are hardwired to respond to negative thoughts. When you consistently focus on your flaws, failures, or fears, your brain starts to believe that these thoughts reflect reality. You may begin to see yourself as inadequate, believing that you'll never be able to succeed or that there's something fundamentally wrong with you.

This constant negativity can wear you down emotionally. It's like carrying a heavy weight around with you all day, every day. Over time, the burden becomes overwhelming. You may find it harder to find joy in activities you once enjoyed, and you may start avoiding social interactions or responsibilities because you feel drained.

Depression often begins with this sense of hopelessness—feeling stuck in a loop of negative thoughts that seem impossible to escape. Anxiety, on the other hand, thrives on fear and worry. When your inner dialogue is full of criticism and doubt, you start to anticipate the worst in every situation. The result? A mind that's constantly racing, worrying about what might go wrong.

Both depression and anxiety feed off persistent negativity. The more you criticize yourself, the more anxious or down you feel, and the more your mental health suffers. But here's an important question: Can you stop this cycle before it spirals out of control?

Recognizing the Warning Signs

The first step to protecting your mental health is recognizing when negative self-talk is becoming a problem. We all experience bad days or moments of doubt, but when those feelings become persistent, it's a sign that something deeper may be going on.

Here are a few warning signs to watch out for:

- **Constant negative thinking**: Are you frequently telling yourself that you're not good enough or that things will never get better?

- **Withdrawal from activities**: Have you stopped doing things you used to enjoy because they feel too overwhelming or pointless?
- **Difficulty concentrating**: Are you struggling to focus because your mind is constantly racing with negative thoughts or worries?
- **Changes in mood**: Do you find yourself feeling sad, irritable, or anxious most of the time?
- **Physical symptoms**: Are you experiencing headaches, fatigue, or trouble sleeping, which may be linked to your mental and emotional state?

If you recognize any of these signs, it's important to take them seriously. Persistent negativity doesn't just affect your mood—it can have long-term consequences for your mental health if left unchecked.

So, what can you do to protect yourself from the effects of negative self-talk?

Steps to Protect Your Mental Health

One of the most effective ways to combat the effects of negative self-talk is to practice mindfulness. Mindfulness involves being present in the moment and observing your thoughts without judgment. When you notice a negative thought creeping in, acknowledge it, but don't let it take over. Instead of engaging with it, simply observe it and let it pass.

For example, if you catch yourself thinking, "I'll never be good enough," pause and take a deep breath. Ask yourself: *Is this thought based on reality, or is it just a reaction to how I'm feeling right now?* More often than not, these thoughts are just fleeting emotions, not facts.

Another helpful tool is reframing. Reframing involves challenging negative thoughts and replacing them with more balanced, positive ones. Let's say you're struggling at work and thinking, "I'm terrible at this job." Instead of accepting that thought as truth, try reframing it: "I'm going through a tough time, but I'm learning and improving." Reframing helps shift your focus from what's wrong to what's possible.

It's also important to take care of your physical health. Regular exercise, a balanced diet, and enough sleep can significantly improve your mood and energy levels. Physical activity, in particular, has been shown to reduce symptoms of depression and anxiety by releasing endorphins, the brain's "feel-good" chemicals.

Finally, don't be afraid to ask for help. If you're feeling overwhelmed by persistent negativity, talking to a therapist or counselor can provide valuable support. Sometimes, it's hard to see a way out when you're in the thick of it, but a professional can help guide you through your thoughts and develop coping strategies to protect your mental health.

Moving Toward a Healthier Mindset

Imagine how different your life could be if you weren't weighed down by constant self-criticism. Picture waking up in the morning without immediately dreading the day ahead, or having the confidence to face challenges without being overwhelmed by doubt. By taking steps to reduce negative self-talk, you can improve your mental health and build a more positive, fulfilling life.

It won't happen overnight, and there will be days when the negative thoughts feel overwhelming. But remember that you have the power to change your inner dialogue. The key is to be patient with yourself, to challenge the negative thoughts, and to replace them with compassion and understanding.

So, ask yourself: What can you do today to start protecting your mental health?

Reflection Questions:

1. How often do you catch yourself engaging in negative self-talk? What kinds of thoughts typically come up?
2. Can you think of a time when persistent negativity affected your mood or behavior?
3. What warning signs have you seen that might point to the impact of negative thoughts on your mental health?
4. How would your life change if you practiced more mindfulness and reframed your negative thoughts?
5. What support systems do you have in place to help you manage stress and anxiety?

Practical Exercise:

For the next week, keep a journal of your negative thoughts. Each time you notice a self-critical or negative thought, write it down. Then, next to it, write a more balanced or positive way of looking at the situation. For example, if you write, "I'll never be able to do this," try replacing it with, "I might struggle at first, but I can learn and get better." Review your journal at the end of the week and reflect on how this practice affected your mood and mental health.

Chapter 7: Affects Physical Health

How Negative Self-Talk Leads to Headaches, Fatigue, and Trouble Sleeping

The Story of Rachel

Rachel had always been someone who pushed herself hard, both at work and in her personal life. She set high expectations for herself and held herself to them relentlessly. But lately, something had been off. She started waking up in the middle of the night, her mind racing with thoughts about all the things she hadn't done right that day. Her neck and shoulders were constantly tense, and no matter how much sleep she got, she woke up exhausted. Worst of all, headaches had become a regular part of her day.

"I'm just not handling things well," Rachel would tell herself. "Why can't I get it together like everyone else?" She didn't realize that this constant stream of negative self-talk was at the root of her physical symptoms.

Have you ever felt like Rachel? You might think that your body's stress—headaches, tiredness, trouble sleeping—is purely a physical issue, but what if your mind is playing a bigger role than you think? Negative self-talk doesn't just affect your emotions; it can take a serious toll on your physical health as well. But how does this happen, and what can you do about it?

How Negative Self-Talk Leads to Physical Symptoms

Our minds and bodies are deeply connected, more than we often realize. When you engage in constant self-criticism, your body reacts as though you're under threat. This triggers a stress response in the brain, releasing hormones like cortisol and adrenaline that are designed to help you deal with danger. These hormones increase your heart rate, tense up your muscles, and sharpen your focus.

In small doses, this stress response can be useful. But when you're constantly engaging in negative self-talk, your body remains in this heightened state of stress for long periods of time, even when there's no real danger. Over time, this chronic stress can manifest as physical symptoms—headaches, muscle tension, trouble sleeping, and fatigue.

Have you ever noticed that when you're stressed or anxious, your body feels different? Your shoulders might feel tight, your head might start pounding, and even though you're exhausted, you can't seem to get a good night's sleep. These are clear signs that your negative thoughts are impacting your physical health.

But why does stress from negative self-talk show up in these particular ways?

Why Stress Causes Headaches, Fatigue, and Sleep Problems

When you engage in self-criticism, the stress response triggers a chain reaction in your body. One of the most common physical symptoms of stress is tension headaches. These headaches are often caused by tightness in the muscles around the neck, shoulders, and scalp—areas that naturally tense up when you're stressed. As the tension builds, it can lead to that familiar, throbbing pain behind your eyes or at the base of your skull.

Fatigue is another common symptom of chronic stress. Even though you may feel mentally drained, your body is working overtime, constantly producing stress hormones that keep you in a state of alertness. This can lead to a cycle where, despite feeling exhausted, you have trouble fully relaxing, which prevents your body from recovering.

Sleep problems often go hand in hand with fatigue. If your mind is filled with negative thoughts and worries—"Why can't I do better?" or "I'm not good enough"—it can be difficult to wind down at night. You may find yourself tossing and turning, your mind racing with everything you did wrong that day. Even if you do fall asleep, the quality of your sleep might be poor, leading to grogginess and more fatigue the next day.

But here's the question: How can you break this cycle of negative self-talk before it causes more damage to your physical health?

What You Can Do to Reduce the Physical Impact of Negative Thoughts

The first step in reducing the physical effects of negative self-talk is to recognize when it's happening. Start by paying attention to your body. Are you feeling tense? Do you have a headache or feel unusually tired? These physical signs can be signals that your mind is stuck in a loop of self-criticism. Once you notice the connection, you can take steps to address both the mental and physical aspects of the problem.

One of the most effective ways to break the cycle is through relaxation techniques. Deep breathing exercises, progressive muscle relaxation, or gentle stretching can help release tension in your muscles and calm your mind. These practices work by sending a signal to your brain that it's okay to relax, which can reduce the flow of stress hormones and help you feel more at ease.

Another powerful tool is mindfulness. By practicing mindfulness, you can train your brain to stay focused on the present moment instead of dwelling on negative thoughts from the past or worries about the future. Mindfulness meditation, for example, involves sitting quietly, focusing on your breath, and observing your thoughts without judgment. Over time, this practice can help you develop a more balanced and compassionate inner dialogue.

Physical activity is also key to managing the physical effects of stress. Regular exercise, whether it's walking, yoga, or any other form of movement, releases endorphins, which are natural mood boosters. Exercise also helps your body burn off excess stress hormones, reducing tension and promoting better sleep.

Improving Sleep Through Self-Compassion

One of the biggest areas where negative self-talk can take a toll is on your sleep. When you go to bed with a head full of self-criticism and worry, it's no surprise that your body has trouble settling down. But what if, instead of letting those negative thoughts keep you awake, you practiced self-compassion?

Before you go to sleep, take a few minutes to reflect on the positive things you accomplished during the day. They don't have to be big—maybe you helped a coworker with a problem, finished a task you'd been putting off, or made a healthy choice. Acknowledge these small victories, and remind yourself that you're doing your best.

It can also help to create a bedtime routine that signals to your body that it's time to unwind. Try turning off screens an hour before bed, dimming the lights, and doing something relaxing like reading or journaling. Writing down your thoughts before bed can help you clear your mind of any lingering worries, making it easier to fall asleep.

The key is to break the cycle of stress and tension before it takes over your body. By practicing self-care and challenging negative thoughts, you can protect both your mental and physical health.

Moving Toward Physical and Emotional Wellness

Imagine how different your body would feel if you weren't subject to constant criticism. Picture waking up in the morning after a full night of restful sleep, your head clear and your body relaxed. How would your day change if you had more energy and less tension?

The good news is that you have the power to change the way you think, and by doing so, you can protect your body from the harmful effects of stress. It starts with being kind to yourself— acknowledging that no one is perfect and that it's okay to make mistakes. By reducing negative self-talk and taking care of your physical health, you can create a positive cycle of wellness that improves both your mind and body.

So, ask yourself: What can you do today to start feeling better, both mentally and physically?

Reflection Questions:

1. When was the last time you experienced physical symptoms like headaches or fatigue? Can you link them to a stressful or negative thought pattern?
2. How does your body feel when you're caught in a cycle of self-criticism? Where do you notice tension or discomfort?
3. What habits or practices could you introduce into your daily routine to help reduce stress and promote relaxation?
4. How would your sleep improve if you practiced self-compassion and let go of negative thoughts before bed?
5. What small changes can you make today to protect your physical health from the effects of stress?

Practical Exercise:

At the end of each day, take five minutes to do a body scan. Sit or lie down in a quiet place, close your eyes, and slowly focus on each part of your body, starting from your head and moving down to your toes. Notice any areas of tension or discomfort. As you breathe in, imagine releasing that tension with each exhale. After your body scan, write down one negative thought you had during the day and replace it with a more positive or balanced perspective. Over time, this practice can help you become more aware of the connection between your thoughts and your body, allowing you to release stress before it builds up.

Chapter 8: Reduces Resilience

How Constant Self-Criticism Makes It Harder to Bounce Back

The Story of Daniel

Daniel had always prided himself on being a hard worker. But recently, things hadn't been going his way. After a failed project at work, he couldn't shake the feeling that he was incompetent. His thoughts spiraled: "I'm just not good enough," "Why do I even bother?" and "Everyone else is better at this than I am."

Each time Daniel encountered a new challenge, he hesitated. Instead of diving in like he used to, he second-guessed himself, convinced that failure was inevitable. When a new project came up, he avoided it. "What's the point?" he'd think. "I'll just mess it up like last time." Over time, Daniel's confidence plummeted, and he found himself giving up before even trying.

Have you ever felt like Daniel? Maybe after a setback or failure, you found it hard to recover. You might have started believing that no matter what you do, it's never enough. When you're stuck in a cycle of self-criticism, your ability to bounce back—your resilience—takes a serious hit. But why does this happen, and what can you do to rebuild your resilience?

How Self-Criticism Erodes Resilience

Resilience is the ability to recover from setbacks, adapt to challenges, and keep moving forward despite difficulties. It's the mental toughness that helps you pick yourself up after a failure and try again. But when you're constantly criticizing yourself, resilience becomes much harder to maintain.

Here's why: Every time you face a setback and respond with self-criticism—"I'm a failure" or "I'll never get it right"—you're reinforcing the idea that you're incapable of improvement. Instead of seeing the setback as an opportunity to learn or grow, you see it as proof that you're not good enough. Over time, this belief makes you more likely to give up, even when the next challenge might have a better outcome.

But here's the question: What if you could see setbacks not as reflections of your worth, but as stepping stones toward growth? How would that change the way you approach challenges?

Why Self-Criticism Leads to Giving Up

When you're overly critical of yourself, failure becomes something to fear. You start associating setbacks with personal flaws rather than viewing them as part of the learning process. This mindset can make even small obstacles feel insurmountable. You might avoid challenges altogether, thinking, "Why try if I'm just going to fail again?"

This fear of failure is rooted in perfectionism. When you believe that nothing less than perfect is acceptable, every mistake feels like a confirmation that you're not good enough. And the more you believe this, the less likely you are to take risks or push yourself outside your comfort zone. But avoiding challenges and giving up too soon prevents you from building the resilience you need to handle setbacks and keep moving forward.

But what if you could change your response to failure? What if, instead of seeing it as proof of inadequacy, you viewed it as a natural part of growth?

Rebuilding Resilience by Changing Your Mindset

The first step to rebuilding resilience is to change the way you think about failure. Instead of letting self-criticism control your response, try shifting your focus to what you can learn from the experience. Every setback, no matter how small, offers an opportunity for growth. The more you embrace this mindset, the more resilient you become.

One way to do this is by practicing self-compassion. When you make a mistake or face a setback, treat yourself with the same kindness you would offer a friend. For example, if a friend failed an exam, you wouldn't say, "You're so bad at this. You'll never get it right." You'd say something like, "It's okay—you'll learn from this and do better next time." Start offering yourself the same encouragement.

Another key to building resilience is reframing how you view setbacks. Instead of thinking, "I failed, so I'm not good at this," try thinking, "I didn't succeed this time, but that doesn't mean I won't improve." This shift in perspective helps you see failure as a temporary setback rather than a permanent reflection of your abilities.

It's also important to break tasks into smaller, manageable steps. When a challenge feels too big, it can be overwhelming, especially if you're already struggling with self-criticism. Breaking it down into smaller goals makes it feel more achievable, and each small success builds your confidence and resilience.

But what about the times when you do face a major setback? How can you stay resilient in the face of big failures?

Learning to Bounce Back from Major Setbacks

Resilience isn't about never failing—it's about getting back up when you do. One of the most important skills you can develop is the ability to look at failures objectively. Instead of focusing on the emotional sting of the setback, ask yourself: *What went wrong, and what can I learn from this?*

For example, if you didn't get the promotion you were hoping for, it's easy to fall into a pattern of self-blame. But instead of thinking, "I'm just not good enough," try analyzing the situation. Was there something specific you could improve? Did you need more experience or a different approach? Viewing failure as a learning experience rather than a personal flaw helps you develop resilience and bounce back stronger.

Another tool for building resilience is setting realistic expectations. No one is perfect, and expecting perfection from yourself will only set you up for disappointment. Instead, focus on progress, not perfection. Celebrate the small victories along the way, and remind yourself that growth takes time.

Most importantly, don't be afraid to ask for help. Resilience doesn't mean you have to go through challenges alone. Reaching out to friends, family, or a mentor for support can give you the perspective and encouragement you need to keep moving forward.

Moving Toward Greater Resilience

Imagine how different your life could be if, instead of giving up after a setback, you saw every challenge as an opportunity to grow. Picture yourself facing obstacles with confidence, knowing that even if things don't go perfectly, you have the strength and resilience to keep trying.

The journey to greater resilience begins with changing the

way you talk to yourself. Instead of letting self-criticism define your response to failure, practice self-compassion, reframe your setbacks, and focus on progress. By doing so, you'll not only build the resilience to bounce back from setbacks but also unlock your full potential for growth and success.

So, the next time you face a challenge, ask yourself: *How can I use this as an opportunity to grow?*

Reflection Questions:

1. When was the last time you faced a setback and immediately criticized yourself? How did it affect your willingness to try again?
2. How would your approach to challenges change if you viewed failure as a stepping stone rather than a dead end?
3. What negative thoughts come up when you think about past failures? How can you reframe them in a more positive, growth-focused way?
4. How do you usually respond when things don't go as planned? What steps can you take to build resilience in those moments?
5. Who can you turn to for support when you're struggling to bounce back from a setback?

Practical Exercise:

The next time you encounter a setback, take a few minutes to write down your immediate thoughts and feelings. Then, challenge those thoughts. For example, if you wrote, "I'll never be able to do this," replace it with, "This didn't work out, but it's a chance to learn and improve." Finally, write down one action you can take to move forward, even if it's a small step. By regularly practicing this, you'll start to build the resilience needed to handle challenges without letting self-criticism hold you back.

Chapter 9: Skews Perception

How Negative Self-Talk Distorts Your Reality

The Story of Laura

Laura had just received a promotion at work. Her boss praised her for her hard work, and her colleagues congratulated her. But as Laura sat at her desk, instead of feeling proud, she felt an overwhelming sense of dread. "It's only a matter of time before they realize I'm not good enough," she thought. "I got lucky this time, but I don't deserve this."

No matter how many compliments or positive feedback she received, Laura couldn't shake the feeling that she wasn't capable. In her mind, every success was diminished, and every challenge felt like an impossible mountain to climb. The problem wasn't her abilities—it was how she perceived them. Negative self-talk had distorted her reality, making her achievements feel meaningless and her challenges seem insurmountable.

Have you ever felt like Laura? You accomplish something great, but instead of feeling proud, you focus on the one thing that didn't go perfectly. Or maybe you're faced with a new challenge, and instead of feeling confident, your mind convinces you that you're bound to fail. This is what happens when negative self-talk skews your perception of reality. But how does this happen, and what can you do to see things more clearly?

How Negative Self-Talk Warps Your Perception

Our thoughts shape the way we see the world. Negative self-talk can significantly distort your perception when it dominates your inner dialogue. You start to believe that your flaws are bigger than they really are, that your successes are insignificant, and that the challenges ahead are too difficult to overcome.

This distorted thinking is often a result of cognitive biases—mental filters that color the way you interpret your experiences. For example, you might fall into the trap of *catastrophizing*, where you blow small problems out of proportion and see them as disasters. Or you might engage in *all-or-nothing thinking*, where you believe you either have to be perfect, or you're a complete failure.

When negative self-talk takes over, it's like wearing a pair of glasses that make everything look darker and more difficult than it really is. But here's an important question: What would happen if you could take off those glasses and see your situation more clearly?

Why Negative Self-Talk Makes Challenges Seem Insurmountable

When you're constantly criticizing yourself, even small challenges can feel overwhelming. Negative self-talk convinces you that you're not capable, that you'll fail, or that it's not worth trying. As a result, you may avoid taking action altogether because the challenge feels too big to handle.

This distorted thinking can turn simple tasks into major sources of stress. For example, if you're asked to give a presentation at work, your mind might immediately jump to thoughts like, "I'm terrible at public speaking. I'll mess this up, and everyone will see that I don't belong here." These kinds of thoughts make the challenge seem impossible, even though you're fully capable of handling it.

But what if you could change the way you think about challenges? What if, instead of seeing them as threats, you saw them as opportunities for growth?

Why Negative Self-Talk Minimizes Your Achievements

Another way negative self-talk skews your perception is by minimizing your achievements. When you accomplish something, instead of celebrating, you may brush it off as "no big deal" or attribute it to luck. You might think, "Anyone could have done that," or "It wasn't as good as it could have been."

This pattern of thinking is known as *discounting the positive*. It's a way of downplaying your successes so that you don't have to acknowledge them. The problem with this is that it robs you of the confidence and motivation that come from recognizing your accomplishments. When you don't allow yourself to feel proud of what you've achieved, it becomes harder to take on new challenges with confidence.

But here's the truth: Your achievements matter, no matter how small they may seem. And learning to recognize and celebrate them is an important part of shifting your perception away from negativity.

Reclaiming a Balanced View of Reality

The good news is that you can change the way you perceive

yourself and your challenges by challenging your negative self-talk. The first step is awareness. Start paying attention to the thoughts that come up when you're faced with a challenge or after you've accomplished something. Are you telling yourself that you're not good enough? Are you downplaying your successes or blowing your problems out of proportion?

Once you're aware of these thoughts, challenge them. Ask yourself: *Is this thought based on facts, or is it just a negative assumption I'm making?* For example, if you think, "I'll never be able to handle this project," ask yourself, "Have I successfully handled similar projects before? What evidence do I have that I can't succeed?"

Another important strategy is to focus on the facts. Instead of letting your mind jump to the worst-case scenario, look at the reality of the situation. If you've accomplished something, acknowledge it without minimizing it. If you're facing a challenge, break it down into smaller, manageable steps and remind yourself of the skills and strengths you already have.

One way to practice this is to keep a "reality check" journal. Whenever you catch yourself engaging in negative self-talk, write down the thought, then write a more balanced or realistic perspective. For example, if you think, "I'm terrible at this," you might write, "I'm not perfect at this yet, but I'm learning and improving."

Building Confidence by Celebrating Success

Celebrating your successes—no matter how small—is a key part of shifting your perception. Instead of brushing off your accomplishments, take a moment to reflect on what you did well. It could be something as simple as finishing a task on time, overcoming a fear, or handling a difficult situation with grace.

The more you acknowledge your successes, the more confident you'll feel in your ability to handle future challenges.

But here's the important part: Don't wait for someone else to validate your achievements. Practice giving yourself credit. You don't need a big, public celebration to recognize your hard work—a simple "I'm proud of what I accomplished today" can go a long way in building a more balanced, positive perception of yourself.

Moving Toward a Clearer, Healthier Perspective

Imagine how different your life would feel if you saw your challenges for what they are—not insurmountable obstacles, but opportunities to learn and grow. Picture yourself recognizing your achievements, not as flukes or luck, but as a result of your hard work and talent. How would your confidence change? How much more motivated would you feel?

By changing the way you talk to yourself, you can begin to see the world—and yourself—more clearly. You'll start to recognize that challenges aren't as overwhelming as they seem, and that your achievements are worth celebrating. Over time, this shift in perception will help you build a healthier, more balanced view of reality.

So, ask yourself: What can I do today to start seeing myself and my challenges more clearly?

Reflection Questions:

1. When faced with a challenge, how often do you assume it's too difficult for you to handle? What thoughts usually come up?
2. How do you react when you accomplish something? Do

you give yourself credit, or do you downplay your success?

3. What cognitive distortions (such as catastrophizing or all-or-nothing thinking) do you notice in your self-talk? How can you challenge them?

4. How would your perception of yourself change if you focused more on your strengths and achievements instead of your flaws?

5. What is one small achievement from today or this week that you can take a moment to celebrate?

Practical Exercise:

For the next week, keep a journal of your achievements, no matter how small. Each day, write down at least one thing you accomplished—whether it's finishing a task at work, being kind to someone, or making progress on a personal goal. At the end of the week, review your entries and reflect on how you felt about each accomplishment at the time. Then, write down a more positive or balanced way to view those achievements. This practice will help you build the habit of recognizing your successes and seeing your challenges more clearly.

Chapter 10: Creates a Negative Cycle

How Negative Self-Talk Becomes a Self-Defeating Loop

The Story of Mia

Mia sat at her desk, staring at the long list of tasks she had yet to finish. It seemed like no matter how hard she worked, there was always more to do. "I'm never going to catch up," she thought. "Why do I even bother? I'm just not good enough to handle all of this."

This wasn't the first time Mia felt overwhelmed. In fact, these thoughts had been creeping into her mind more and more lately. Every time she faced a new challenge, her inner critic jumped in, telling her she wasn't capable. As time went on, these thoughts became louder, stronger, and harder to shake. Each day felt like a battle to get through, and Mia couldn't remember the last time she felt truly proud of something she accomplished. The cycle of negativity had taken over.

Have you ever found yourself in a similar loop? Maybe you start the day with a sense of dread, already anticipating that things won't go well. Each time something doesn't go perfectly, it feels like confirmation of what you already believe: that you're not good enough. This is how a cycle of negative self-talk can trap you. But how does this cycle start, and more importantly, how can you break free from it?

How Negative Self-Talk Becomes a Vicious Cycle

Negative self-talk doesn't usually start as a full-blown habit. It often begins with a small, critical thought—maybe after you make a mistake or experience a setback. "I'm not good at this," you tell yourself. At first, this might seem harmless. But over time, if left unchecked, these small negative thoughts grow into a pattern.

Every time you face a challenge or encounter a new obstacle, the negative thoughts resurface, reinforcing the belief that you're not capable. This, in turn, affects how you respond to new situations. You might start avoiding challenges or giving up easily because you've convinced yourself that you'll fail anyway. The more you engage in this type of thinking, the more deeply ingrained it becomes.

It's like walking along a dirt path. Each time you take the same route, you wear the path down a little more. Eventually, that path becomes so well-worn that it's hard to step off and create a new one. Negative self-talk works the same way—the more you engage in it, the more automatic it becomes, and the harder it is to change your thinking.

But here's the question: What if you could step off that well-worn path? What if you could break the cycle and create a new, healthier way of thinking?

Why the Cycle Is Hard to Break

Breaking the cycle of negative self-talk can feel difficult because it's self-reinforcing. Each time you engage in negative thinking, you're more likely to interpret future situations through the same negative lens. For example, if you tell yourself, "I'm bad at my job," you might start noticing every little mistake you make, while ignoring the things you do well. This selective attention only strengthens the belief that you're not capable.

In this way, negative self-talk becomes a self-fulfilling prophecy. The more you believe you'll fail, the more likely you are to give up, avoid trying, or perform poorly—all of which reinforce the original negative thought. This creates a vicious cycle where negativity feeds on itself, making it harder and harder to break free.

But here's the good news: Even though this cycle feels powerful, it's not unbreakable. With practice and persistence, you can begin to shift your thinking and stop negative self-talk in its tracks.

What You Can Do to Break the Cycle

The first step in breaking the cycle of negative self-talk is awareness. Start by paying attention to the thoughts that run through your mind during difficult or stressful moments. Are your thoughts harsh, self-critical, or defeatist? Once you recognize these negative patterns, you can begin to challenge them.

One effective way to challenge negative thoughts is by questioning their accuracy. Ask yourself: *Is this thought really true, or am I jumping to conclusions?* For example, if you think, "I always mess things up," take a step back and look for evidence. Is it really true that you always fail, or is it just your frustration speaking in the moment? By challenging your negative thoughts, you can start to weaken their hold over you.

Another powerful tool for breaking the cycle is to replace

negative self-talk with more balanced or positive thoughts. This doesn't mean forcing yourself to be overly optimistic—it's about being realistic and fair with yourself. Instead of thinking, "I'm terrible at this," try reframing the thought: "I'm still learning, and it's okay to make mistakes." Replacing negative thoughts with more compassionate ones can help shift your mindset over time.

It's also helpful to practice self-compassion. When you make a mistake or face a setback, instead of beating yourself up, treat yourself with kindness. Remind yourself that everyone makes mistakes and that setbacks are a natural part of growth. By being kinder to yourself, you'll find it easier to break the cycle of negativity and bounce back from challenges.

Why Breaking the Cycle Improves All Areas of Your Life

Negative self-talk doesn't just affect one part of your life—it can seep into every area, from your work to your relationships to your personal goals. When you're stuck in a negative cycle, you're more likely to doubt your abilities, avoid challenges, and miss out on opportunities for growth. You might also become more sensitive to criticism, more withdrawn in your relationships, and less confident in pursuing your goals.

But when you break the cycle, everything starts to change. By shifting your inner dialogue from negative to more balanced, you begin to approach challenges with a sense of possibility instead of dread. You're more willing to take risks, try new things, and learn from your experiences. Your relationships improve because you stop assuming the worst about yourself and how others see you. And, most importantly, you start to believe in your own potential again.

Imagine what your life could look like if, instead of tearing yourself down, you built yourself up. How much more resilient, confident, and motivated would you be if you didn't let negative self-talk run the show?

Moving Toward a More Positive, Empowered Mindset

Breaking the cycle of negative self-talk isn't easy, but it's possible. It starts with small steps—becoming more aware of your thoughts, challenging them when they're unfair, and replacing them with more compassionate, realistic perspectives. The more you practice, the less power those negative thoughts will have over you.

As you begin to step off the well-worn path of self-criticism and create a new path of self-compassion, you'll notice a shift in how you see yourself and your abilities. Challenges that once felt overwhelming will become manageable, and you'll find that you're more willing to take risks and learn from setbacks. Over time, this new cycle of positivity will begin to reinforce itself, making it easier to maintain a healthy, empowered mindset.

So, ask yourself: What would your life look like if you broke the cycle of negative self-talk and started believing in yourself again?

Reflection Questions:

1. When you face challenges or setbacks, what kind of negative self-talk do you typically engage in? How does it affect your behavior?
2. Can you think of a time when negative self-talk became a self-fulfilling prophecy? How did that impact the outcome?
3. What steps can you take to challenge and reframe negative

thoughts when they arise?

4. How would your life change if you replaced negative self-talk with self-compassion and encouragement?

5. What is one area of your life that the cycle of negative thinking has affected? How can you start to shift your mindset in that area?

Practical Exercise:

For the next week, keep a "negative thought log." Each time you catch yourself engaging in negative self-talk, write down the thought and what triggered it. Then, challenge the thought by asking: *Is this thought really true? What's a more balanced or compassionate way to think about this situation?* Write down the new, more positive thought. At the end of the week, review your log and reflect on how your thinking has changed. This practice will help you break the cycle of negativity and develop a more supportive inner dialogue.

Now WHAT? You May Ask.

So, you've recognized how negative self-talk is holding you back. You've read about the ways it damages your confidence, affects your relationships, and even harms your physical and mental health. But now, you might be wondering: *Now what? Where do I go from here?* It's a fair question, and one that many people ask when they start confronting the negative voices in their heads.

At this point, you may feel a little overwhelmed. After all, changing the way you talk to yourself isn't a switch you can just flip. It's a process, and like any process, it takes time, patience, and effort. But here's the good news: You don't have to overhaul your entire mindset overnight. In fact, small steps can lead to big changes. But what should those steps be?

Let's start with the most important one—awareness. You've probably noticed that negative self-talk often creeps in without you even realizing it. One minute you're going about your day, and the next, you're stuck in a loop of self-criticism. So, the first step is simply to notice when it happens. Pay attention to the moments when you feel your mood drop or when a small setback spirals into feelings of failure. What are you saying to yourself in those moments?

Once you're aware of these thoughts, the next step is to challenge them. This might feel strange at first—after all, we're so used to believing our thoughts without question. But just because you think something doesn't make it true. Ask yourself: *Is this thought based on reality, or is it just a reaction to how I'm feeling in the moment?* Often, you'll find that your thoughts are exaggerated or overly critical.

So, what do you do once you've recognized and challenged your negative thoughts? You replace them. This doesn't mean you have to force yourself into being overly positive—it's about being balanced and fair. Instead of thinking, "I'm terrible at this," you might say, "I'm still learning, and that's okay." It's not about denying your challenges; it's about acknowledging them without letting them define you.

But you might be asking yourself, *Will that really make a difference?* It's a valid question, especially if you've been stuck in a cycle of negativity for a long time. The answer is yes. Little by little, the way you talk to yourself shapes the way you see yourself. Think of it like planting seeds. Every time you choose a kinder thought, you're planting a seed for a more compassionate, confident version of yourself to grow.

Of course, it's one thing to know these strategies in theory, but how do you put them into practice in your everyday life? One simple approach is to start small. Set aside a few minutes at the end of each day to reflect on your thoughts. Were there moments when you caught yourself being overly critical? How could you have responded differently? Writing these reflections down can help solidify the habit of noticing and challenging negative thoughts.

Another practical step is to create a mantra or phrase that you can turn to when self-doubt creeps in. It could be something as simple as, "I'm doing my best" or "I'm learning every day." The key is to choose something that feels genuine to you—something you can believe in, even when things don't go perfectly.

But here's the thing: As you begin this process, there will be days when it feels like nothing is changing. You might slip back into old patterns, and that's okay. Changing your mindset isn't a straight path; it's more like a series of hills and valleys. On the tough days, remind yourself that progress isn't about being perfect—it's about being consistent. Each time you catch a negative thought and replace it with a kinder one, you're taking a step forward, even if it feels small in the moment.

Now you might be wondering, *What about the deeper changes?* After all, replacing a few thoughts here and there is helpful, but how do you build a long-lasting, positive relationship with yourself? The answer lies in making self-compassion a habit. Self-compassion means treating yourself with the same kindness and understanding you would offer to a close friend. It's about giving yourself grace when things go wrong, instead of tearing yourself down.

One way to cultivate self-compassion is by practicing gratitude. At the end of each day, write down three things you're grateful for. These don't have to be huge—they could be as simple as appreciating a sunny day or a kind word from a friend. Over time, focusing on gratitude helps shift your attention from what's going wrong to what's going right, even on difficult days.

Another powerful tool is to surround yourself with supportive people. We all need a little encouragement sometimes, and the people we spend time with can either lift us up or bring us down. Take stock of your relationships. Are there people in your life who constantly criticize or belittle you? If so, it might be time to set some boundaries. On the flip side, spend more time with people who believe in you, who remind you of your strengths, and who encourage you to keep going when things get tough.

So, where does all this lead? You may be asking yourself, *What's the end goal here?* The answer is simple: to build a healthier, more compassionate relationship with yourself. To reach a point where, instead of being your harshest critic, you become your greatest supporter. It's about trusting that you have the ability to handle whatever life throws at you—not because you're perfect, but because you're resilient, adaptable, and constantly growing.

Now, as you take these first steps toward changing the way you talk to yourself, remember: it's not about fixing everything all at once. It's about progress, not perfection. So, what will your next step be?

That's the question you need to ask yourself: *Now what?* It's time to decide. Will you continue the same path, letting negative self-talk control your life, or will you take that first step toward a new, kinder way of thinking? The choice is yours—and you're more capable of making it than you realize.

Conclusion: A Final Word of Thanks

First and foremost, thank you for buying this book and taking the time to read it. The fact that you made it to the end of this journey speaks volumes about your desire to change the way you talk to yourself, to break free from the patterns of negativity that have been holding you back, and to embrace a healthier, more compassionate relationship with yourself.

Writing this book has been a deeply personal and meaningful experience, and I hope that the words within these pages have resonated with you. Changing how we speak to ourselves is not easy, but every small step you take toward kindness and self-compassion is a victory worth celebrating. You deserve to live a life free from the weight of negative self-talk, and I'm grateful to have been part of your journey toward that goal.

Now, as you move forward, remember that this is a process—one that will take time and patience. There will be days when it feels challenging, and there will be moments when you doubt yourself. But every time you choose to counter a negative thought with a kinder one, you are rewriting the story you tell yourself. And that story? It's one of growth, strength, and resilience.

Before we part ways, I have a small favor to ask: If this book has been helpful to you in any way, I'd love for you to leave a review. Not only would your feedback mean the world to me, but your review can also help others who may be struggling with the same issues you've worked through. Sometimes, all it takes is a single review to inspire someone to pick up a book they desperately need to read.

By leaving a review, you're not just supporting me—you're helping spread an important message of hope and self-compassion to countless others who may feel trapped in their own cycles of negative self-talk. Your words can make a difference and might just be the encouragement someone else needs to take that first step toward a more positive and empowered life.

Thank you once again for allowing me to be part of your journey. I wish you all the best as you continue to grow, thrive, and embrace the strength within you. Remember, you are capable of so much more than you realize. Now, it's time to go out there and show the world—and yourself—just how powerful you can be.